What Are Lakes?

by Mari C. Schuh

Consulting Editor: Gail Saunders-Smith, Ph.D.
Consultant: Sandra Mather, Ph.D., Professor Emerita,
Department of Geology and Astronomy,
West Chester University,
West Chester, Pennsylvania

Pebble Books

an imprint of Capstone Press
Mankato, Minnesota

Pebble Books are published by Capstone Press
1710 Roe Crest Drive, North Mankato, Minnesota 56003
www.capstonepub.com

Library of Congress Cataloging-in-Publication Data
Schuh, Mari C., 1975–
    What are lakes? by Mari C. Schuh.
    p. cm.—(Earth features)
    Includes bibliographical references (p. 23) and index.
    Summary: Photographs and simple text introduce the features of lakes.
    ISBN-13: 978-0-7368-1170-5 (hardcover)
    ISBN-10: 0-7368-1170-2 (hardcover)
    ISBN-13: 978-0-7368-4455-0 (softcover pbk.)
    ISBN-10: 0-7368-4455-4 (softcover pbk.)
    1. Lakes—Juvenile literatures. [1. Lakes.] I. Title. II. Series.
GB1603.8 .S38   2002
551.48′3—dc21   2001004842

Note to Parents and Teachers

The Earth Features series supports national science standards for
units on landforms of the earth. The series also supports geography
standards for using maps and other geographic representations.
This book describes and illustrates lakes. The photographs support
early readers in understanding the text. The repetition of words and
phrases helps early readers learn new words. This book also
introduces early readers to subject-specific vocabulary words, which
are defined in the Words to Know section. Early readers may need
assistance to read some words and to use the Table of Contents,
Words to Know, Read More, Internet Sites, and Index/Word List
sections of the book.

Printed in the United States of America in North Mankato, Minnesota.
042013
007305R

Table of Contents

A lake is water
surrounded by land.

Glaciers once covered parts of the earth. Melting ice from the glaciers formed many lakes.

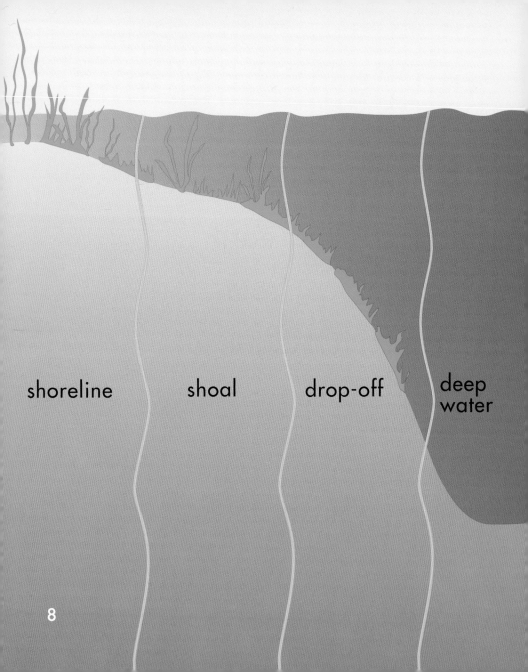

shoreline   shoal   drop-off   deep water

A lake has four zones.

Some lakes are small
and some lakes are big.

12

Big lakes have
waves. Small lakes
have no waves.

Some lakes are shallow
and some lakes are deep.

Sand covers some lake bottoms. Mud and weeds cover other lake bottoms.

Some lakes are saltwater lakes. Some lakes are freshwater lakes.

Great Salt Lake in northwestern Utah

North
America

Lake Superior

Lake Superior is in North America. Lake Superior is the largest freshwater lake in the world.

Words to Know

deep—going a long way below the surface of the water

freshwater—water that does not have salt; most lakes are freshwater lakes.

glacier—a huge mass of slowly moving ice; glaciers often form in high mountain valleys where snow never completely melts.

Lake Superior—a large lake that borders Minnesota, Michigan, and Wisconsin in the United States, and Ontario in Canada; Lake Superior is 31,820 square miles (82,414 square kilometers) in area.

saltwater—water that has a lot of salt and other minerals in it; water in oceans and some lakes is saltwater.

wave—a moving ridge on the surface of water

zone—an area that is separate from other areas

Read More

Chambers, Catherine. *Lakes.* Mapping Earthforms. Chicago: Heinemann Library, 2000.

Levete, Sarah. *Rivers and Lakes.* Closer Look At. Brookfield, Conn.: Copper Beach Books, 1999.

Morris, Neil. *Rivers and Lakes.* Wonders of Our World. New York: Crabtree, 1998.

Owen, Andy, and Miranda Ashwell. *Lakes.* Geography Starts. Des Plaines, Ill.: Heinemann Interactive Library, 1998.

Internet Sites

FactHound offers a safe, fun way to find Internet sites related to this book. All of the sites on FactHound have been researched by our staff.

Here's all you do:

Visit *www.facthound.com*

FactHound will fetch the best sites for you!

Index/Word List

Word Count: 92
Early-Intervention Level: 15

Credits

Kia Bielke, cover designer; Jennifer Schonborn, production designer and
   interior illustrator; Kimberly Danger and Jo Miller, photo researchers

Comstock, Inc., 1
David Jensen, cover, 14
Frederick Atwood, 4
James P. Rowan, 12 (top)
John Elk III, 12 (bottom), 16 (bottom), 18
Photo Network/Bachmann, 6; Dennis Mac Donald, 10 (bottom)
Tom Stack/TOM STACK & ASSOCIATES, 20
Visuals Unlimited/Larry Mellichamp, 10 (top); Betty Sederquist, 16 (top)

The author dedicates this book to her hometown of Fairmont, Minnesota,
known as "The City of Lakes."